For my two baby bumblebees,
Leah and Hailey.
You inspire me!

Kelly Hastings

For Bethann and Family,
who know firsthand that
the bee story is indeed true.

Alan St. Jean

© Text copyright 2020 Alan St. Jean.
© Illustrations copyright 2020 Kelly Hastings.
All rights reserved. First Edition.
Published by Oren Village, LLC, Sunbury, Ohio.
For information or permission to reproduce, please contact
alanstjean@gmail.com or write to Alan St. Jean, PO Box 900, Sunbury, Ohio 43074.
Text set in Anime Ace 2.0.
Cover design by Lilla Hangay. Illustrations were digitally rendered.

Names:
St. Jean, Alan, author. | Hastings, Kelly, illustrator.
Title:
Chased by a bee! / by Alan St. Jean & Kelly Hastings.
Description:
First edition. | Sunbury, Ohio : Oren Village, LLC, [2020] | Series: The young authors collection ; v. 4. | Audience: children. | Summary: A country boy and his dog were visiting a park one day when they were confronted by a great, big bee! It was scary! A chase ensued, there was tragedy and there was triumph from the unlikeliest of heroes in this heartwarming tale about a simple misunderstanding.--Publisher.
Identifiers:
ISBN: 978-1-7333020-3-6
Subjects:
LCSH: Bees--Juvenile fiction. | Dogs--Juvenile fiction. | Miscommunication--Juvenile fiction. | Heroes--Juvenile fiction. | Children's stories. | CYAC: Bees--Fiction. | Dogs--Fiction. | Miscommunication--Fiction. | Heroes--Fiction. | LCGFT: Picture books.
Classification:
LCC: PZ7.S14245 C53 2020 | DDC: [Fic]--dc23

Oren Village

Chased by a Bee!

by Alan St. Jean
and Kelly Hastings

The Young Authors Collection • Volume 4

I'M GONNA TELL YOU A STORY, THIS MAY BE HARD TO BELIEVE.
I CAN'T EXPLAIN IT, BUT I CAN'T CONTAIN IT, SOMETHIN' SCARY HAPPENED TO ME.

A scary thing, happened to me!

"HEY, I'LL TELL THE STORY."

A scary thing, Happened to me!

"STOP!"

"UGH!"

MINDIN' MY BUSINESS ON A SUNNY DAY. TOOK OL' BLUE TO THE PARK, LET HER OUT TO PLAY.

THE BIRDS WERE SINGIN', LEANED AGAINST A TREE

WHEN I SAW TWO EYES, STARIN' AT ME!

I SAW BLACK AND YELLA,	IT STARTED BUZZIN' AROUND.	A GIANT BUMBLEBEE, OH WHAT A FRIGHTFUL SOUND!
I JUMPED TO MY FEET	AND WHISTLED FOR BLUE,	WE MET AT THE TRUCK AND WITH MY SHOE...

I STEPPED ON THE GAS, TORE DOWN THE ROAD.

SWERVED TO THE RIGHT, JUST MISSED A TOAD!

THE TRUCK WAS SPEEDIN', BUT TO MY SURPRISE...

GOIN' SIXTY FIVE, TWO BIG BLACK EYES!

A bumblebee,
HEY,
is chasing me!
IT'S MY STORY!
A bumblebee,
UGH!
is chasing me!
LIKE I WAS SAYIN'...

MADE A RIGHT TURN DOWN AN OLD DIRT ROAD

TO THE FISHIN' HOLE, WHEN I SAW THAT TOAD.

HE WAS HOPPIN' ALONG LIKE A KANGAROO, COVERED IN MUD LIKE DIPPITY DOO!

FLIES WELCOME HE WAS SINGIN' AND SCREAMIN', HIS BREATH WAS BAD...	LIKE A ROTTEN CHIMICHANGA IN A COWBOY HAT!
WITH ALL THE DISTRACTIONS, I HIT A BIG ROCK,	WENT FLYIN' THROUGH THE AIR PAST A BUNCH OF LIVESTOCK.

THEN THAT GREAT BIG BEE DID THE CRAZIEST THING, IT CAUGHT ME IN THE AIR BY A LOOP IN MY JEANS!

I SAW THE BIG STINGER

AND THE EYES

AND THE CLAWS!

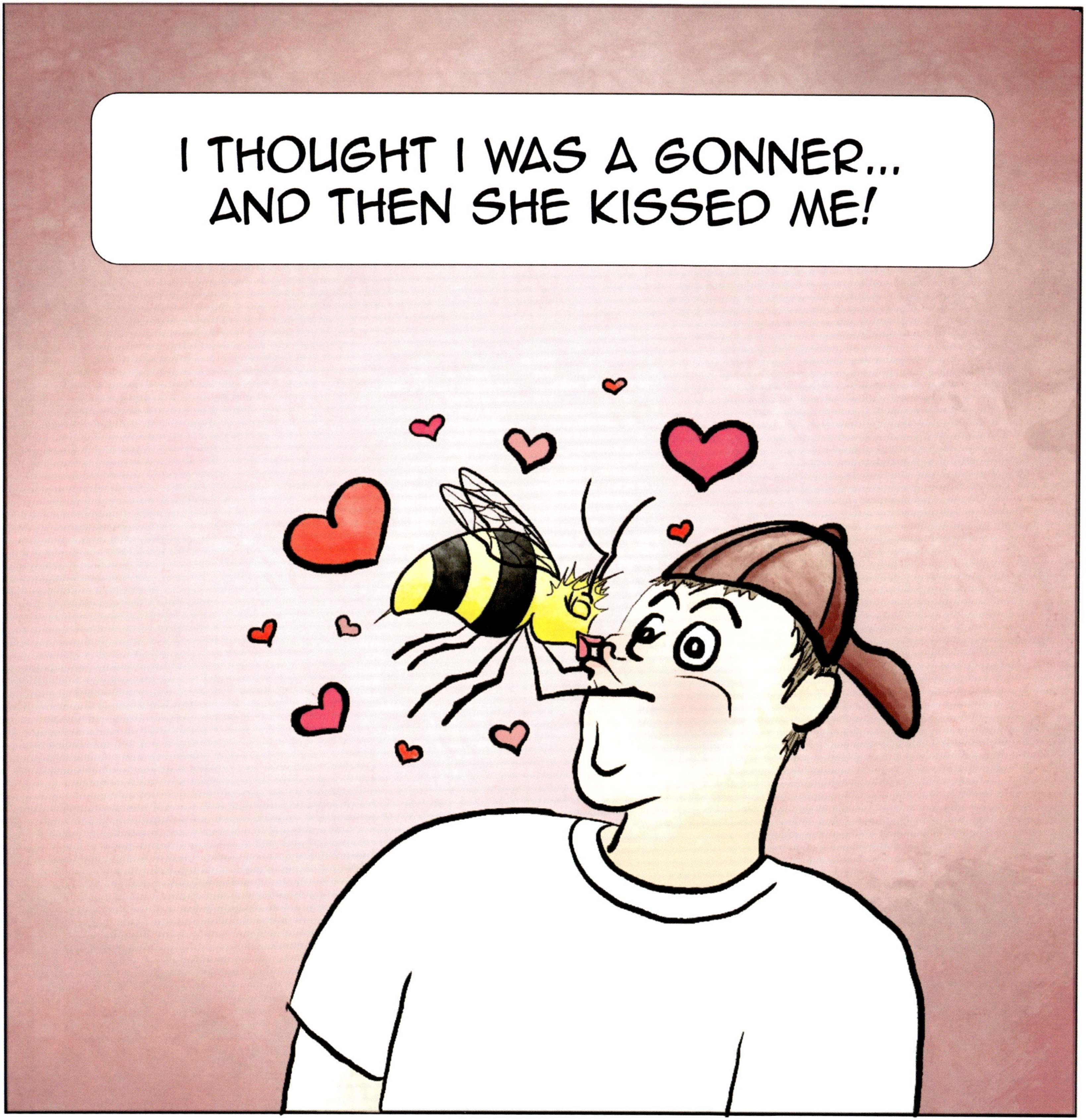
I THOUGHT I WAS A GONNER...
AND THEN SHE KISSED ME!

A bumblebee,
YUCK!
is chasing me!
SHE'S KINDA PRETTY!
A bumblebee,
THAT'S ME...
is chasing me!
MY TURN!

LITTLE DID HE KNOW, WAY BACK IN THE PARK, WHEN HE LEANED AGAINST THE TREE AND OL' BLUE BARKED...

A BIG HAIRY SPIDER HAD DISCOVERED MY NEST!

MY BABIES WERE IN DANGER, I WAS ALL DISTRESSED!

WHEN HIS BACK HIT THE TREE,

THE SPIDER WAS SQUASHED!

THAT WHITE T-SHIRT IS GONNA NEED WASHED!

WHEN I TRIED TO THANK HIM, HE DROVE QUICKLY AWAY. SO I FOLLOWED ALONG, I JUST HAD TO SAY

Panel 1: HOW HAPPY AND LUCKY AND THRILLED I WAS,

Panel 2: BUT ALL HE COULD HEAR WAS A BUZZ BUZZ BUZZ.

Panel 3: WHEN HE HIT THE BIG ROCK AND FLEW UP IN THE AIR,

Panel 4: I COULDN'T LET HIM FALL. HE LOOKED SO HANDSOME!

Panel 1:

A bumblebee, is chasing me!

"SHE KISSED ME!"

"ARE YOU SURE?"

Panel 2:

A bumblebee, is chasing me!

"OF COURSE I'M SURE!"

"I DON'T KNOW..."

BEFORE THIS TALE COULD BECOME A LOVE STORY,

A BAD THING HAPPENED, IT WAS REALLY GORY!

THE TOAD STUCK OUT HIS TONGUE, WITH A GREAT BIG SLURP, HE SWALLOWED THAT BEE...

FOLLOWED BY A BURP!

BURP

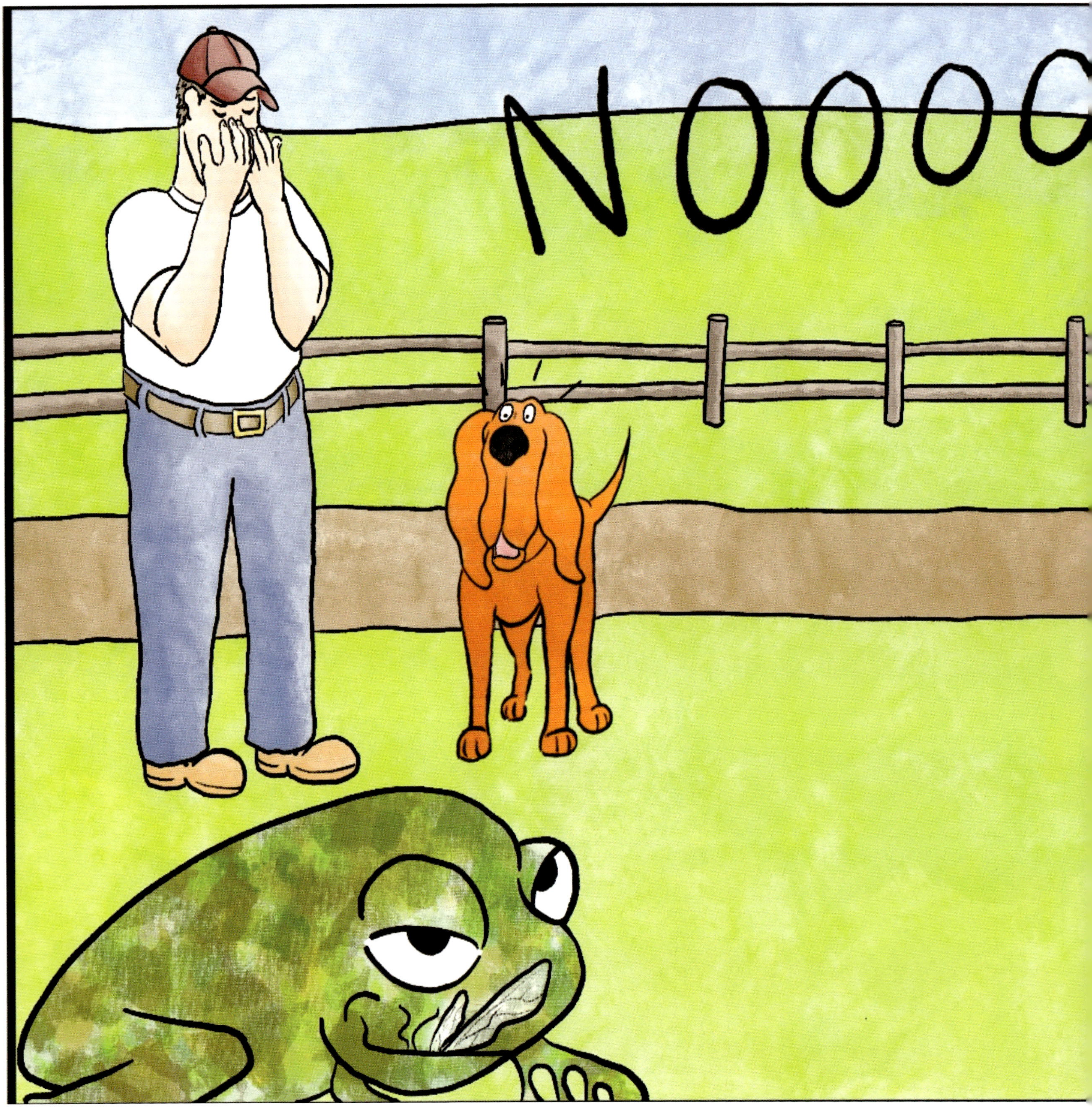
NOOOO

OOOOOOOOO!

NOW I'VE NEVER BEEN A HERO, I'VE ALWAYS WALKED AWAY, BUT THE BABIES WERE A CRYIN' 'CAUSE THEIR MAMA WAS AN ENTREE.

I WHISTLED REAL LOUD, MY DOG CAME A RUNNIN',

I POINTED AT THE TOAD AND HOLLERED,

HOWWW!

'BLUE! DO SOMETHIN'!'

THAT SWEET OL' HOUND DOG GROWLED A GROWL. HE WAS COMIN' FOR THE TOAD, HE WAS ON THE PROWL!

THE TOAD JUMPED HIGH, BUT BLUE JUMPED HIGHER,

THREW HIM IN A PAN, PUT HIM OVER A FIRE.

IF ANYONE TELLS YOU THAT TOADS CAN'T SCREAM, JUST TAKE IT FROM ME IT'S LIKE YOUR SCARIEST DREAM. AND WHEN HE SCREAMED THAT BEE WAS OUTED. THE MAMA WAS SAVED, HER BABIES SHOUTED!

A bumblebee,
THANK YOU.
is chasing me!
WASN'T NUTHIN'.

A bumblebee,
YOU'RE SO NICE!
is chasing me!
I GOTTA GO!

I WAS DRIVIN' HOME
AS THE SUN WENT DOWN,
BUZZ Z Z Z
WHEN TO MY SURPRISE
I HEARD A BUZZIN' SOUND.
AN ITTY BITTY BUG,
A BABY BUMBLEBEE!
YOU GOTTA BE KIDDIN'!

I'M BRINGIN' HOME A BABY BUMBLEBEE!

THAT WAS FUN! THANKS FOR READING ALONG!

NOW, LET'S WATCH THE MUSIC VIDEO!

YOU CAN WRITE A STORY, TOO!

WRITING A STORY IS NOT HARD. IN FACT, IT'S A LOT OF FUN!
I'VE PROVIDED SPACE FOR YOU TO CREATE A STORY OF YOUR VERY OWN!
YOU'RE GOING TO BE AN AUTHOR AND AN ILLUSTRATOR!
FIRST, LET'S JOT SOME IDEAS DOWN SO WE KNOW HOW TO BEGIN.

1. WHERE DOES YOUR STORY HAPPEN? (SETTING)

ANSWER HERE

2. WHAT IS YOUR MAIN CHARACTER'S NAME?

ANSWER HERE

WHAT KIND OF STORY DO YOU THINK THIS WILL BE?
CHECK THE BOX OR BOXES THAT YOU THINK FITS BEST:
(GENRE)

- [ ] ACTION
- [ ] SCIENCE FICTION
- [ ] WESTERN
- [ ] NON FICTION
- [ ] COMEDY
- [ ] MYSTERY
- [ ] FOLK TALE
- [ ] SCARY
- [ ] ROMANCE

HELPFUL HINTS
(DON'T WORRY, OUR FRIENDS WILL HELP AS YOU GO.)

WHEN YOU WRITE:
ADD DETAILS, LIKE:
- WHAT IS YOUR CHARACTER DOING?
- WHY ARE THEY DOING IT?
- HOW ARE THEY FEELING?

WHEN YOU DRAW:
*DRAW YOUR PICTURE WITH A PENCIL FIRST SO YOU CAN MAKE CHANGES EASILY.
*THEN, COLOR IT!
(THAT'S HOW ILLUSTRATORS DO IT)
*ALSO, ADD DETAILS! SHOW THE SURROUNDINGS. BE CREATIVE!

ARE YOU READY TO START??

LET'S MEET YOUR CHARACTER

IN THIS SCENE, DRAW A NICE, BIG PICTURE OF YOUR CHARACTER. BE SURE TO USE A LOT OF DETAIL BECAUSE WE'RE INTRODUCING THEM TO THE READER. THIS IS THEIR PHYSICAL APPEARANCE.

IN THE BUBBLE BOX, TELL US TWO THINGS ABOUT YOUR CHARACTER. ARE THEY GOOD, OR BAD? ARE THEY HAPPY, OR SAD? ARE THEY SILLY, OR ARE THEY SNEAKY? THINGS LIKE THAT. THIS HELPS US INDERSTAND YOUR CHARACTER'S PERSONALITY.

Thing one:

Thing two:

LET'S START THE STORY: BEGINNING

USE THE BUBBLE BOX TO WRITE THE BEGINNING OF YOUR STORY, THEN DRAW A PICTURE TO BRING YOUR WORDS TO LIFE. MAKE SURE YOU DRAW THEIR SURROUNDINGS, TOO. FOR EXAMPLE, IF THEY'RE IN A JUNGLE, DRAW TREES AND JUNGLE STUFF. IT'S CALLED THE SETTING. DETAILS ARE WHAT MAKE PICTURES AWESOME! DON'T TRY TO DRAW LIKE ANYONE ELSE, JUST DRAW THE WAY YOU DRAW, IT'S YOUR STYLE AND IT IS GOOD ENOUGH! YOU'RE AN ILLUSTRATOR!

One day,

PLOT: THE BIG 'WHY'

WHAT HAPPENS NEXT IN YOUR STORY? DRAW THE SCENE HERE. IN THE BUBBLE BOX, EXPLAIN WHAT IS HAPPENING AND TELL US WHY THE CHARACTER IS DOING WHAT THEY ARE DOING.

Then,

CONFLICT: SOMETHING GOES WRONG

THINGS ARE ABOUT TO GET BAD. CONFLICT HELPS MAKE A STORY MORE INTERESTING. BASED ON WHAT'S HAPPENING IN THE STORY, TELL US WITH A PICTURE AND WITH YOUR WORDS WHAT HAS GONE WRONG FOR YOUR CHARACTER. ALSO, TELL US HOW THE CHARACTER FEELS ABOUT THE CONFLICT. THIS HELPS THE READER CONNECT WITH THE STORY.

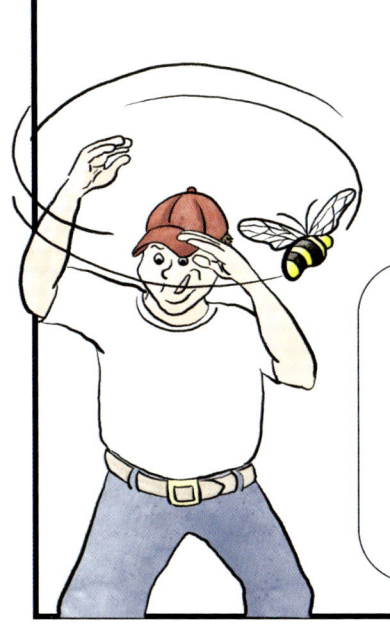

Suddenly,

MORE CONFLICT!

OH, NO! AS IF THINGS WEREN'T BAD ENOUGH, SOMETHING ELSE WENT WRONG! THIS IS AWFUL! WAIT A MINUTE. HMMM. NO, THIS IS FUN!

Things got worse because

RESOLUTION

CONFLICT IS FUN IN A STORY, BUT WE NEED TO FIX THE PROBLEM SO THAT THE READER FEELS SATISFIED AT THE END. IF WE DON'T FIX THE PROBLEM, THE STORY IS NO FUN TO READ.
DRAW A PICTURE AND USE YOUR WORDS TO TELL US WHAT HAPPENS NEXT THAT CAN FIX THE PROBLEMS FOR YOUR CHARACTER. DO THEY FIGURE OUT A WAY TO FIX THEIR OWN PROBLEM?
OR, DID SOMEONE ELSE SAVE THEM?

The day was saved when

ENDING

WE'RE NOT SIMPLY GOING TO SAY 'THE END' HERE...THAT'S SILLY AND MAKES THE STORY WAY TOO SHORT. LET'S HAVE FUN WITH THIS. IN THE BUBBLE BOX, TELL US WHAT YOUR CHARACTER LEARNED FROM THEIR EXPERIENCE. THEN, DRAW A PICTURE THAT SHOWS WHAT BECAME OF THEM IN THE FUTURE! DID THEY BECOME FAMOUS? DID THEY GET MARRIED? I KNOW...EWWW!

Our character learned